DiscoverRoo
An Imprint of Pop!
popbooksonline.com

History's Greatest Mysteries

HISTORY'S MOST BAFFLING SIGHTINGS

by Grace Hansen

abdobooks.com

Published by Pop!, a division of ABDO, PO Box 398166, Minneapolis, Minnesota 55439.

Printed in the United States of America, North Mankato, Minnesota.

052022
092022

THIS BOOK CONTAINS RECYCLED MATERIALS

Cover Photos: Shutterstock Images

Interior Photos: Shutterstock Images; Getty Images; AP Image Collection; Army Air Force Intelligence; Garrick Mallery; David G. Baker; Kenneth C. Zirkel

Editor: Elizabeth Andrews
Series Designer: Candice Keimig

Library of Congress Control Number: 2021951860

Publisher's Cataloging-in-Publication Data

Names: Hansen, Grace, author.

Title: History's most baffling sightings / by Grace Hansen

Description: Minneapolis, Minnesota : Pop, 2023 | Series: History's greatest mysteries | Includes online resources and index

Identifiers: ISBN 9781098242282 (lib. bdg.) | ISBN 9781644947913 (pbk.) | ISBN 9781098242985 (ebook)

Subjects: LCSH: Unidentified flying objects--Sightings and encounters--Juvenile literature. | Unidentified flying objects--Juvenile literature. | Curiosities and wonders--Juvenile literature.

Classification: DDC 130.973--dc23

WELCOME TO DiscoverRoo!

Pop open this book and you'll find QR codes loaded with information, so you can learn even more!

Scan this code* and others like it while you read, or visit the website below to make this book pop!

popbooksonline.com/baffling-sightings

*Scanning QR codes requires a web-enabled smart device with a QR code reader app and a camera.

TABLE OF CONTENTS

CHAPTER 1

BRAVE OR FOOLISH?

People may fear sharing their baffling stories because of other people's reactions. The teller might be called an attention-seeker or even insane. In some cases, a shot at 15 minutes of fame is enough for a person to make up a tall

WATCH A VIDEO HERE!

tale. Few have been brave enough to share their experience and stick by it, even if it brought them endless **ridicule**.

Photographer Frank Searle claimed to have captured a photo of the Loch Ness Monster in Scotland, but it was later found to be a fake.

CHAPTER 2

BIGFOOT BELIEVERS

Bigfoot and creatures like it have been talked about around the world for centuries. The beasts go by different names, but witness descriptions are mostly the same: they are very large, hairy, humanlike, and shy. There are

LEARN MORE HERE!

The Yokuts Tribe of California left behind paintings of "Hairy Man" that are likely 500 to 1000 years old.

numerous recorded sightings. Though most have been **debunked**, others cannot be explained. The most famous sighting to date is also the most debated.

Bob (left) and Roger compare casts they made of Bigfoot footprints.

October 20, 1967 was a beautiful fall day in northern California. Cowboys and friends Roger Patterson and Bob Gimlin were riding horseback in the Six Rivers National Forest. They were in the area to investigate recent sightings of Bigfoot tracks. Bob was **skeptical**. He didn't really believe something like a Bigfoot could exist. Roger, on the other hand, was very excited. He wanted to capture one on video and share the proof with the world.

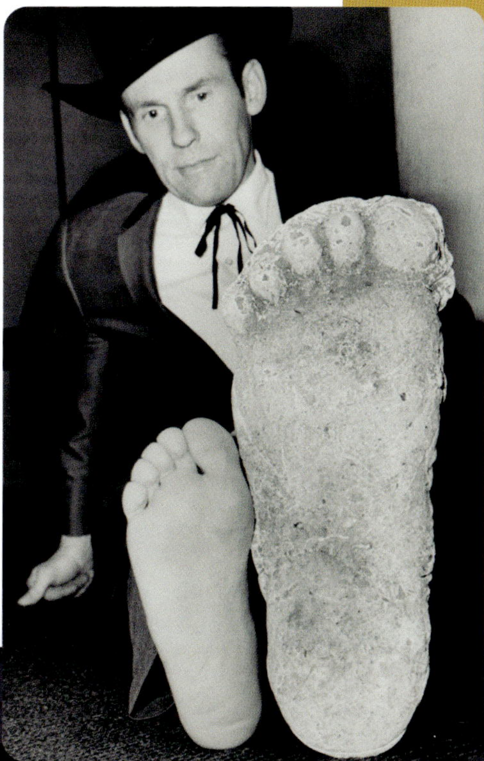

Roger shows the difference in size between his foot and a Bigfoot's.

The men followed old logging roads deep into the forest. They came up to a creek. Suddenly, Roger's horse got spooked. It jumped and lunged. Bob's horse did the same. There was an overpowering odor in the air. Then they laid eyes on what their horses sensed. It was a Bigfoot!

Roger fumbled for his video camera. Luckily, the creature tripped as it hurried away. Roger began filming. The creature righted itself and continued on. For a moment, the Bigfoot

A still shot from the famous footage of the Bigfoot looking over its shoulder.

turned its head to look back at the men, and then disappeared into the forest.

BIGFOOT FACTS

DID YOU KNOW?

Bob Gimlin and his family were harassed by people who did not believe him. So he refused to talk publicly about his experience for 35 years.

Since that fateful day, the famous footage has been viewed millions of times by both skeptics and believers. Some of those believers are scientists. For them, the evidence points to an **elusive** creature closely related to humans and apes that has yet to be identified. Former doubter Bob Gimlin has just one complaint about the brief recording: "...that ain't nothin'. I saw a lot more than that."

CHAPTER 3

NINE FLASHES OF LIGHT

On a clear day on June 24, 1947, Kenneth Arnold flew his CallAir A-2 at 9,200 feet (2,804m) over Mineral, Washington. A flash of light reflected off his windshield. Arnold feared he was too close to another aircraft. He scanned the sky but could

COMPLETE AN ACTIVITY HERE!

only identify a plane about 15 miles (24km) behind him. It couldn't have caused the light he saw.

Kenneth Arnold standing in front of his CallAir in 1947

Then several flashes of light, nine to be exact, shone in the distance. Arnold got a closer look. The flashes came from flying objects. He described them as crescent shaped. They moved like "saucers skipping over water." They flipped, **banked**, and darted around in perfect unison. He thought they were a new type of military aircraft. But

Pilots, including Arnold (middle), *look at a photo of a unidentified flying object (UFO).*

An image of a UFO captured by a hiker in New Mexico on March 12, 1967.

these did not give off tails behind them. They also flew very fast—around 1,700 miles per hour (2,736kph). That was much faster than any other aircraft at the time.

When the objects flew in front of Mount Rainier, they appeared dark against the snowcapped mountain. Soon, they were gone. At 4:00 pm, an hour after the encounter, Arnold landed in Yakima, Washington. He shared his story there, and it quickly spread.

DID YOU KNOW?

The **Pentagon** released a report in June of 2021. It identified 143 cases of what it called UAEs—or Unidentified Aerial Phenomena—since 2004 that could not be explained. However, the government also found no evidence of alien life.

People respected Arnold, a well-known businessman and pilot. Many took him seriously. What's more, other people saw the same flying objects. Several reports came from the exact area around the same time. The most **compelling** account came from a United Airlines flight 10 days later. The plane was over

Idaho when its crew noticed nine flying objects following them.

An investigation by the Army Air Force and Federal Bureau of Investigation (FBI) began on July 9. Three weeks later, it was concluded that what people witnessed was not imaginary. But it also couldn't be explained.

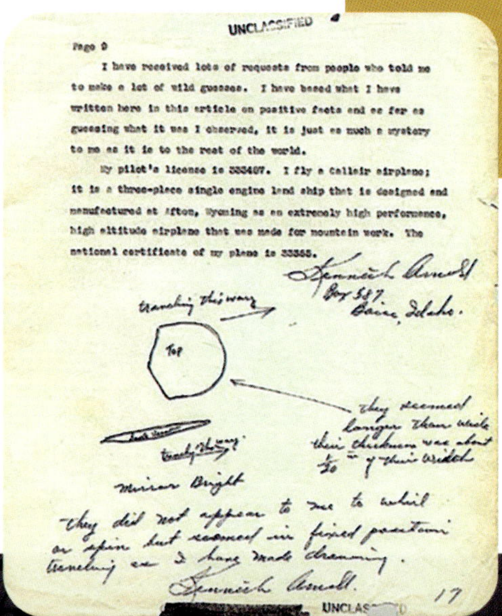
UNCLASSIFIED

Page 9

I have received lots of requests from people who told me to make a lot of wild guesses. I have based what I have written here in this article on positive facts and as far as guessing what it was I observed, it is just as much a mystery to me as it is to the rest of the world.

My pilot's license is 333487. I fly a Callair airplane; it is a three-place single engine land ship that is designed and manufactured at Afton, Wyoming as an extremely high performance, high altitude airplane that was made for mountain work. The national certificate of my plane is 33355.

Kenneth Arnold
Box 587
Boise, Idaho.

traveling this way

Top

they seemed longer than wide their thickness was about 1/20 of their width

traveling this way

mirror Bright

they did not appear to me to whirl or spin but seemed in fixed position traveling as I have made drawing.

Kenneth Arnold.

UNCLASSIFIED

Arnold writes that he cannot make a guess as to what he saw, and draws an image of the UFO.

CHAPTER 4

LOST TIME

On September 19, 1961, newlyweds Barney and Betty Hill were returning home from a quick honeymoon in Montreal and Niagara Falls. They stopped at a diner in Vermont for coffee. At 10:00 pm they hit the road again. They estimated they'd be

EXPLORE LINKS HERE!

The Hills were an American couple who claimed they were abducted by aliens.

home to Portsmouth between 2:00 and 3:00 am on the 20th. The drive that was supposed to take four hours took seven.

As the Hills drove through the night, they noticed a light following them. At first they thought they were seeing things. Barney stopped the car and Betty grabbed binoculars. Barney said it must be a satellite or a falling star. Through the binoculars Betty saw an object spinning in the air. "Barney, if you think that's a satellite or a star, you're being ridiculous," she told him.

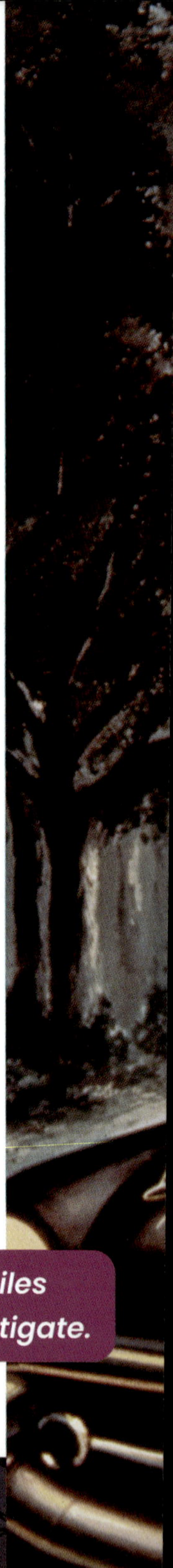

The Hills were followed for miles before they stopped to investigate.

Barney drove on, but the light stayed with them. He again pulled over, grabbed the binoculars, and ran into a field. "My God," Barney said to himself as he looked up in disbelief, "what is this thing? It can't be real." The thing was a giant, round, and flat aircraft. Gray-skinned beings in uniforms stared down from it. Barney

An image of the landscape drawn by David G. Baker from the Hills' description.

An image of the aliens drawn by David G. Baker from the Hills' description.

ran back to the car yelling in fear. He jumped into the driver's seat. Extremely loud sounds rang in the air. The couple lost consciousness. They came to around two hours later, miles from where they last remembered.

For weeks, Betty had very **vivid** dreams. Barney developed anxiety that made him sick. The watches they wore that night never worked again. The Hills went to psychiatrist Benjamin Simon for help. Simon put the couple under **hypnosis** to help them recall what had happened. They slowly pieced the night together.

The giant aircraft landed on their car. The Hills walked up a large ramp into the vessel. One at a time they were taken into a room with curved walls. They sat on a cold metal table. A light beamed down on them. The gray beings took hair, skin, and nail samples from the Hills. They poked them with needles. The beings could communicate with the Hills but spoke a different language to each other. They were not mean. They did something so the Hills would forget their experience and sent them back to the car.

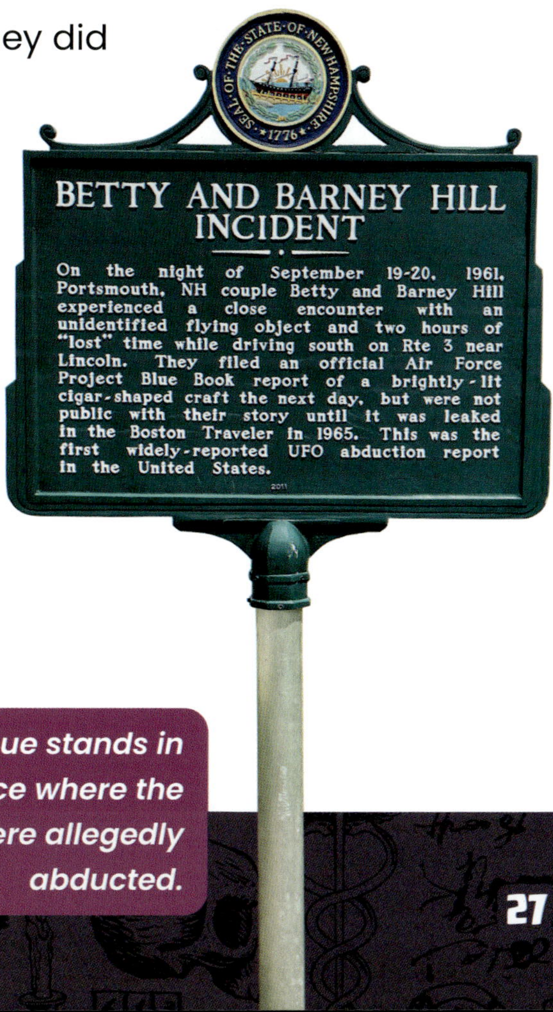

A plaque stands in the place where the Hills were allegedly abducted.

REMOVABLE TEETH

At one point, the gray beings ran into the room where Betty was. They were excited. They had discovered that Barney's teeth could come out of his mouth. They wanted to see if hers did the same. She laughed and explained that her husband had **dentures**. The beings learned about what can happen when humans age.

The Hills never wavered from their story. And no one else on Earth can confirm or deny what happened that September night.

Barney shares a drawing of what he saw in the early hours of September 20, 1961.

MAKING CONNECTIONS

TEXT-TO-SELF

Would you share your story if you saw something unexplainable? Why or why not?

TEXT-TO-TEXT

Have you read any other books about unexplained sightings? What did those stories have in common with the stories in this book?

TEXT-TO-WORLD

Is it important for people to be skeptical about stories of the unexplained? Why would it be important to also keep an open mind?

GLOSSARY

bank – to tip left or right. Banking makes the plane turn. The plane tilts, or banks, as it turns.

compelling – convincing.

debunk – to expose the falseness of a claim.

denture – a partial or complete set of artificial teeth.

elusive – hard to find or catch.

hypnosis – a condition like sleep.

Pentagon – the US Department of Defense.

ridicule – to make fun of or laugh at in an unkind way.

skeptical – having or showing doubt.

vivid – strong, clear images in the mind.

INDEX

ONLINE RESOURCES

popbooksonline.com

Scan this code* and others like it while you read, or visit the website below to make this book pop!

popbooksonline.com/baffling-sightings

*Scanning QR codes requires a web-enabled smart device with a QR code reader app and a camera.